J   Heinrichs, Ann
428.2
HEI   Punctuation

Punctuation

By Ann Heinrichs

THE CHILD'S WORLD®
CHANHASSEN, MINNESOTA

Published in the United States of America by The Child's World®
PO Box 326, Chanhassen, MN 55317-0326
800-599-READ
www.childsworld.com

Content Adviser:
Kathy Rzany, MA,
Adjunct Professor,
School of Education,
Dominican University,
River Forest, Illinois

Photo Credits: Cover/frontispiece: Robert Essel NYC/Corbis. Interior: Corbis: 11 (Ariel Skelley), 13 (Duomo), 14 (Joe McDonald), 21 (Mark Tuschman), 29 (Norbert Schaefer); Getty Images: 17 (Stone/Kathi Lamm), 25 (Photodisc/K Sanchez/Cole Group); Getty Images/Taxi: 5 (David Sacks), 7 (Ken Chernus), 9 (Bernard Jolivalt), 27 (Olivier Ribardiere); PhotoEdit: 19 (Susan Van Etten), 22 (Frank Siteman).

The Child's World®: Mary Berendes, Publishing Director

Editorial Directions, Inc.: E. Russell Primm, Editorial Director; Katie Marsico, Project Editor and Line Editor; Matt Messbarger, Editorial Assistant; Susan Hindman, Copyeditor; Sarah E. De Capua and Lucia Raatma, Proofreaders; Peter Garnham, Elizabeth Nellums, Olivia Nellums, Daisy Porter, and Will Wilson, Fact Checkers; Timothy Griffin/IndexServ, Indexer; Cian Loughlin O'Day, Photo Researcher; Linda S. Koutris, Photo Editor

The Design Lab: Kathleen Petelinsek, Art Direction; Kari Thornborough, Page Production

Library of Congress Cataloging-in-Publication Data
Heinrichs, Ann.
  Punctuation / by Ann Heinrichs.
      p. cm. — (The magic of language)
  Includes index.
  ISBN 1-59296-432-X (lib. bdg. : alk. paper)
  1. English language—Punctuation—Juvenile literature. I. Title.
  PE1450.H367 2006
  428.2—dc22   2005004004

Table of Contents

CHAPTER ONE

STOP THAT THOUGHT!

W hat is a period? It's just a little dot. But it's a very important punctuation mark. It shows where a sentence ends.

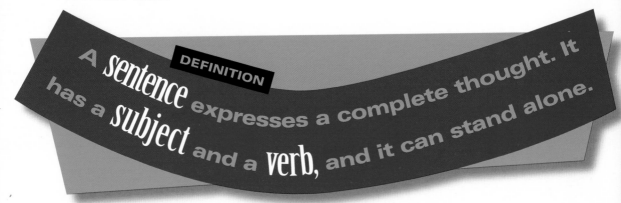

DEFINITION

A **sentence** expresses a complete thought. It has a **subject** and a **verb**, and it can stand alone.

Without periods, all your thoughts would run together. No one could tell what you meant. Just look at this example:

EXAMPLE

Sparky is growling now I wonder why the moose ran away

Sparky is growling because he wants you to use proper punctuation.
A period shows where a sentence ends.

That's pretty confusing! Who is doing what? When and why are they doing it? You need periods to create complete sentences and to show where each thought ends. Here are some ways to do that:

Sparky is growling now. I wonder why. The moose ran away.
Sparky is growling. Now I wonder why. The moose ran away.
Sparky is growling. Now I wonder why the moose ran away.

WATCH OUT!
Never use a comma between two complete sentences!

WRONG Bring the dog in, it's raining.

RIGHT Bring the dog in. It's raining.

WRONG I can't get out, I'm stuck.

RIGHT I can't get out. I'm stuck.

Periods also come after abbreviations. Abbreviations are shortened forms of words.

ABBREVIATION	SHORT FOR
Mr.	Mister
Dr.	Doctor
St.	Street or Saint

*She's **Doctor** Sarkis, but it's easier to use an abbreviation and write **Dr.** Sarkis.*

TRY THESE!

Add **periods** to turn these word groups into **sentences.**

1. Here comes Nicky look at that he's got a new suit

2. Try this gum it's new you'll like it

3. The tiger sneaks up suddenly, he pounces

See page 32 for the answers. Don't peek!

CHAPTER TWO

ASK ME A QUESTION

EXAMPLE

Why can't you clean your room?
When will those robin eggs hatch?
Where did the kangaroo go?

All these sentences are questions. As you can see, a question gets its own punctuation mark. It's a question mark, of course!

You can ask a question with just one or two words. Even short questions get question marks.

EXAMPLE

Who?   **When?**   **Where?**   **Why not?**   **What for?**

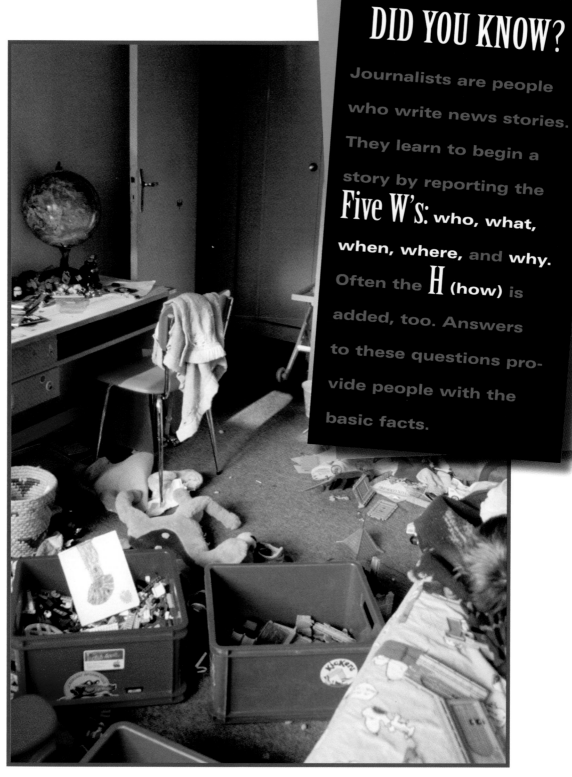

Who made this mess? What were they thinking? When will they clean it up? Where did they go? Why did this happen?

CHAPTER THREE

THE PERFECT MARK FOR YELLING

EXAMPLE

Hey! Wow! Yum! Yuck! Hurray!

All these words are interjections. They grab attention or express feelings. When you say these words, you might even be yelling. Interjections are often followed by an exclamation point.

The words below get exclamation points, too. But watch out! They're not interjections. They're verbs, or action words.

EXAMPLE

Stop!
Help!
Look!
Wait!

RULE

An **exclamation point** is used after a word or **sentence** that expresses strong feelings.

Suppose you say something surprising, shocking, or full of feeling. Then you use an exclamation point.

EXAMPLE

It rained for ten days in a row!
Skippy swallowed his ball!
I just love you, Aunt Jane!

Strong commands get exclamation points, too.

EXAMPLE

Get that lizard out of here!
Eat your vegetables, or else!

That iguana licked my face! I need an exclamation point to emphasize how disgusted I am!

CHAPTER FOUR

LET ME INTRODUCE YOU

Sometimes a group of words introduces the main part of a sentence. These introductory words must be set apart with a comma.

If they want to win, they have to be tough. If they want good grades, they have to put a comma after an introductory group of words.

You might introduce a sentence with just one word. Put a comma after that word.

Gee, **I didn't know you were sleeping.**
Meanwhile, **all the cows escaped.**
Still, **we can bring them back home.**

You might introduce a sentence with a clause. Put a comma after that clause.

DEFINITION

A clause is a group of words that contains a subject and a verb but isn't always a sentence.

If we want to win, **we have to be tough.**
Because he bites, **Lurch must be on**
   a leash.

You could also introduce a sentence with a phrase. That phrase needs a comma, too.

DEFINITION

A *phrase* is a group of words that doesn't include both a **subject** and a **verb.**

After a meal of blackberries, my turtle is happy. *After a phrase,* I use a comma.

Without blackberries, my turtle is sad.

To get A's, Chris has to keep studying.

Whispering softly, she snuggled up to the kitten.

WATCH OUT!

An introductory phrase describes the word that follows it. Never separate the phrase from the word it describes!

WRONG Barking his head off, John put Spot to bed.

RIGHT Barking his head off, Spot went to bed.

WRONG With a sniffle, the mouse was buried.

RIGHT With a sniffle, Susie buried the mouse.

CHAPTER FIVE

MUST YOU INTERRUPT?

Sometimes extra words appear in the middle of a sentence. These words interrupt the flow of the sentence. They must be set apart with commas.

EXAMPLE

Broccoli, for example, is good for you.
Daniel, however, refuses to eat it.

Sometimes the added words explain something or give more information.

EXAMPLE

Uncle Jack, who is ninety years old, loves to swim.
Nicholas, when he feels like it, can be very sweet.

Appositives are set apart by commas, too. An appositive is a word or phrase that explains another word. An appositive usually comes immediately after the word it explains.

Mr. Barrett, our coach, says we should go to bed early.
Whiskers, John's cat, is staring at the bird.

*Whiskers, **a hungry cat**, is quite interested in Perky, **a scared bird**. This sentence has two appositives.*

CHAPTER SIX

KEEPING THINGS APART

Commas do a good job of keeping things apart. For example, a sentence may contain a series, or list. It could be a series of words, phrases, or clauses. If the series has three or more items, a comma separates those items.

EXAMPLE

Our flag is red, white, and blue.
Search in the dog house, under the bed, and on the roof.
Roses are red, violets are blue, and frogs are green.
Please bring cookies, cake, candy, pie, or fudge!

As you see, a conjunction comes before the last item.

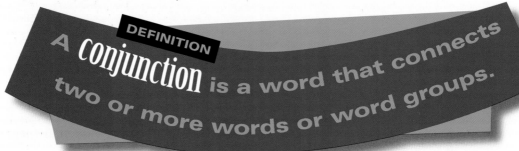

DEFINITION
A conjunction is a word that connects two or more words or word groups.

WATCH OUT!

Some experts say it's okay to leave out the **comma** that comes before the **conjunction**. But this can often make a **sentence** confusing or unclear. Look at the examples on page 18 and imagine them without the final **comma**. Do you still think they are clear?

Did you know that several countries have a flag that's red, white, and blue?

An *independent clause* is a complete thought. It has a **subject** and a *verb*, and it can stand alone.

Every *sentence* contains at least one *independent clause.* Every *independent clause* could be a *sentence.*

Sometimes a sentence contains two independent clauses joined by a conjunction. You usually separate these clauses with a comma. But if the clauses are short, you don't need the comma.

Bozo was good at juggling, but his somersaults were a total flop.
My hands are full of Play-Doh, and my head is full of dreams.
Ride your bike or stay home.

CHAPTER SEVEN

OWNERS AND MISSING LETTERS

What's an apostrophe? You can see one in the last sentence—just look at **What's.** An apostrophe looks just like a comma. The difference is where you place it. An apostrophe is placed near the top of a letter, and a comma is placed near the bottom.

When do you use an apostrophe? Let's start with contractions. A contraction combines two words by leaving some letters out. An apostrophe stands in place of the missing letters.

What's that? It's a shark! Let's take a picture!

EXAMPLE

TWO WORDS	CONTRACTION
what is	what's
it is	it's
we will	we'll
you would	you'd
do not	don't
let us	let's

Possessives need apostrophes, too. A possessive word shows who owns something. Add 's to show the possessive form of a singular word.

Maya's turtle   **the student's homework**
Matt's puppy   **the monkey's tail**

What if there's more than one owner? First, make the word plural.

Usually a plural word ends with s. Then, just add an apostrophe after the s.

*Matt's puppy is snooping around in the **neighbors'** yard. **Matt's** is a singular possessive word. **Neighbors'** is a plural possessive.*

the bunnies' hutches   **the teachers' apples**
the Smiths' house   **the elephants' trunks**

What if the plural doesn't end with *s*? Then add the *'s* at the end.

EXAMPLE

PLURAL	POSSESSIVE PLURAL
children	**the children's lunches**
women	**the women's cars**
mice	**the mice's nest**

TRY THESE!

Use an **apostrophe** to change these word pairs into **contractions.**

1. you are
2. do not
3. should not
4. could have
5. he is
6. who is

See page 32 for the answers. Don't peek!

WATCH OUT!

Never use an **apostrophe** to create a **plural noun!**

WRONG   Bring some snail's and put them in pail's.

RIGHT   Bring some snails and put them in pails.

CHAPTER EIGHT

MAKE THAT CONNECTION

A hyphen is a tiny straight line. It's used to connect words that belong together. For example, it can connect two words acting as a single adjective.

DEFINITION

An **adjective** is a word that modifies, or describes, a noun.

EXAMPLE

Leonardo DiCaprio is a well-known actor.
I can only take chocolate-covered pills.
Your car is at a four-way stop.

A hyphen also connects the two parts of a compound number.

EXAMPLE

Thirty-nine kids ate twenty-three pizzas in fifty-seven seconds!

Some prefixes get hyphens, too.

A **prefix** is a letter or group of letters added to the beginning of a word.

EXAMPLE

The ex-president brought self-rising muffins to the all-American games.

*Our class made these **self-rising** muffins with **all-purpose** flour. The prefixes **self-** and **all-** are always followed by a hyphen.*

CHAPTER NINE

YOU CAN QUOTE
ME ON THAT

Quotation marks have many uses. For one, they enclose quotations. Quotations are someone's exact words.

EXAMPLE

Jack snarled, "Give me a break!" "All I want is some peace," sighed Mom.

Quotation marks also enclose titles of poems and songs.

Anton howled, "Why won't my bunny eat its carrots?" His question is enclosed in quotation marks because those are his exact words.

Can you recite *"Mary Had a Little Lamb"*?
We had to sing *"Row, Row, Row Your Boat"*
for ten minutes.

Sometimes a word is used in an unusual way. Maybe it suggests that

something's not exactly true. Or maybe the word is unfamiliar. In either of

these situations, enclose the word in quotation marks.

Janna brought her *"friend"* **to school. It was**
a tree frog.
With these new *"rules,"* **no one knows what**
to do.
What is this *"zone"* **Joe keeps talking about?**

Quotation marks also enclose translations from another language.

Adiós **is Spanish for** *"good-bye."*
Basta! **is Italian for** *"enough already!"*

CHAPTER TEN

GET THOSE WORDS OUT OF THE WAY!

Like quotation marks, parentheses come in pairs. They enclose words that are in the way. These words might explain something. They might give extra information. They might add a quick thought. But they are not necessary for understanding what's being said.

*Everyone (**except Snoopy**) loves my hamster. He does lots of tricks (**unless it's time to eat!**).*

My best friend (besides Sparky) is Melissa.

Mr. Javier forgot to watch the clock (hurray!), so we had extra time for the exam.

Sarah's hamster (my brother calls it a rat) can do lots of tricks.

As you see, parentheses can enclose a word, a phrase, or a whole sentence. They can also enclose abbreviations, dates, or numbers.

The United Nations (UN) meets in New York City.

Abraham Lincoln (1809–1865) was the sixteenth president.

Our victory in the baseball game was a real squeaker (4–3).

Be sure to bring (1) a fishing pole, (2) some worms, and (3) a bucket.

Congratulations! By now **(if you paid attention),** you're an expert on punctuation!

How to Learn More

At the Library

Hall, Fiona, and Tessie Bundick (illustrator). *The Birth of Finney.* Minnetonka, Minn.: Kasdan Publishing, 2001.

Hope, Dr., Tim Anders (editor), and Richard Pinson (illustrator). *Punctuation Pals.* Fallbrook, Calif.: Alpine Publishing, 1999.

Pulver, Robin, and Lynn R. Reed. *Punctuation Takes a Vacation.* New York: Holiday House, 2003.

Terban, Marvin. *Punctuation Power!: Punctuation and How to Use It.* New York: Scholastic, 2000.

On the Web

Visit our home page for lots of links about grammar:

http://www.childsworld.com/links

NOTE TO PARENTS, TEACHERS, AND LIBRARIANS: We routinely check our Web links to make sure they're safe, active sites—so encourage your readers to check them out!

Through the Mail or by Phone

To find the answer to a grammar question, contact:

THE GRAMMAR HOTLINE DIRECTORY
Tidewater Community College Writing Center, Building B205
1700 College Crescent
Virginia Beach, VA 23453
Telephone: (757) 822-7170

NATIONWIDE GRAMMAR HOTLINE
University of Arkansas at Little Rock, English Department
2801 South University Avenue
Little Rock, AR 72204-1099
Telephone: (501) 569-3161

Fun with Punctuation

Punctuation makes a big difference. It can change the meaning of what you say. The word groups below can have two different meanings. Rewrite each word group twice, using different punctuation to show the two meanings.

1. Help Aaron put a worm on my desk

2. The door is closed why can't I go in

3. Why should I lie down with dogs

4. The carpenter hammers nails and staples

5. Give me three more extra pounds don't bother me

6. She knows that Larry likes me

See page 32 for the answers. Don't peek!

Index

Answers

Answers to Text Exercises
page 7
1. Here comes Nicky. Look at that. He's got a new suit.
2. Try this gum. It's new. You'll like it.
3. The tiger sneaks up. Suddenly, he pounces.

page 23
1. you're
2. don't
3. shouldn't
4. could've
5. he's
6. who's

Answers to Fun with Punctuation
1. Help! Aaron put a worm on my desk.
   Help Aaron put a worm on my desk.
2. The door is closed. Why? Can't I go in?
   The door is closed. Why can't I go in?
3. Why should I lie? Down with dogs!
   Why should I lie down with dogs?
4. The carpenter hammers, nails, and staples.
   The carpenter hammers nails and staples.
5. Give me three more. Extra pounds don't bother me.
   Give me three more extra pounds. Don't bother me!
6. She knows that. Larry likes me.
   She knows that Larry likes me.

About the Author

Ann Heinrichs was lucky. Every year from grade three through grade eight, she had a big, fat grammar textbook and a grammar workbook. She feels that this prepared her for life. She is now the author of more than 180 books for children and young adults. She has also enjoyed successful careers as a children's book editor and an advertising copywriter. Ann grew up in Fort Smith, Arkansas, and lives in Chicago, Illinois.